The
Accidental
Camper

DEER LAKE

The Accidental Camper

H.J. Lewis

Vanwell Publishing Limited
St. Catharines, Ontario

Vanwell Publishing acknowledges the financial support of the Government of Canada through the Book Publishing Industry Development Program for our publishing activities.

Vanwell Publishing acknowledges the Government of Ontario through the Ontario Media Development Corporation's Book Initiative.

Vanwell Publishing Limited
P.O. Box 2131
1 Northrup Crescent
St. Catharines, ON
Canada   L2R 7S2
sales@vanwell.com
1-800-661-6136

Produced and designed by Tea Leaf Press Inc.
www.tealeafpress.com

Cover illustration: Dave Calder

Printed in Canada

National Library of Canada Cataloguing in Publication

Lewis, Jane, 1971–
    The accidental camper / H.J. Lewis.

(Deer Lake, ISSN 1702-0603)
ISBN 1-55068-119-2

    I. Title. II. Series: Deer Lake (St. Catharines, Ont.)

PS8573.E9764A33 2003   C813'.6   C2003-905510-8

*To the Hunt/Strzalkowski/Verge contingent
for the northern experiences*

Chapter 1

"I don't know why *anyone* would want to go canoeing. *Or* camping." Diana Standing held out her hand. She looked at her perfect red fingernails. "You'd get so dirty. And sleeping on the ground..." She shivered. "That *can't* be comfortable."

The girl sitting beside Diana rolled her eyes. "Oh, yeah, Diana. You'd hate camping. You might break a nail."

Mel Randall took a sip of her strawberry milk shake. She looked across the table at her two friends, Diana and Allison. Diana was more her neighbor than her friend. But Diana and Allison were both fourteen. They were the only girls Mel's age in Deer Lake this summer. Mel wanted the three of them to get along.

Diana looked at Allison's hand, which was resting on the table. "You know, you should take better care of your nails," Diana told her.

Allison's dark eyes flashed. "I have more important things to do with my time." She picked up her milk shake and slurped it loudly.

Mel sighed. *Maybe this wasn't such a good idea*, she thought. *I shouldn't have invited them to Charlie's ice cream shop.* She toyed with a lock of her shoulder-length brown hair. *I wanted them to get to know each other. Not start a fight!*

Diana and Allison were both new to Deer Lake this summer. Diana's family bought the cottage next to the Randalls. Allison's cottage was not far away. Her family owned a small shop called the General Store.

Deer Lake was Mel's summer home. The Randall family came here every year. Mel loved it. She wanted Diana and Allison to love it, too.

Mel had met Allison first. The two of them hit it off right away. They both loved canoeing and being outdoors.

Then Mel met Diana. Diana was interested in things like boys and clothes. She was different from Mel and Allison. But she was nice, and she and Mel got along pretty well.

Diana and Allison didn't hit it off at all. They hadn't even tried to be friends. Diana dressed in cute, matching clothes. Allison dressed in rough outdoor gear. Diana liked to read fashion magazines. Allison read books about canoeing and hiking. Both girls had long, straight, dark hair. That was pretty much the only thing they had in common.

Mel was tired of hanging out with one friend at a time. She spent one day with Allison. Then she spent the next day with Diana. *It's silly*, Mel thought to herself. *We should just all hang out together.*

Mel watched Diana and Allison across the table. The two girls stared angrily at each other. *What should I do?* Mel wondered. *I know they are different. But why can't they be friends?*

Allison slurped her shake again. Diana tapped her fingers on the table. No one spoke.

Great, Mel thought to herself. *Now they're not speaking.* She looked around the room. *What can we talk about?* She saw a guy standing inside the front door of Charlie's. He was reading the signs and flyers taped up on the wall.

Mel had a boyfriend, Will Bergeron. She wasn't interested in the guy by the door. But Diana would be! "Hey, look at that cute guy!" Mel said.

Diana's head spun around. Allison rolled her eyes, but she turned around to look.

The guy was tanned and looked strong. He wore hiking boots and brown shorts. His T-shirt had a canoe on it. He had wavy, sandy-colored hair. He looked about sixteen.

"*Hello*," said Diana, smoothing her hair. "I'll take an order of him, with fries on the side."

Allison looked back at Mel. "Who is that?"

"I don't know," said Mel. "He must be new to Deer Lake. Or else he's just visiting."

The girls watched as the guy taped a piece of paper to the wall. Then he left the store. Mel could see him through the front window of Charlie's. He stood on the sidewalk, looking up and down the street.

Diana jumped up and ran to the front door.

"What is she doing?" Allison asked. Diana yanked a piece of paper off the wall. Then she ran back to the table. She slapped the piece of paper down. "I had to see what he was posting," she said.

BAILEY BAY INN SUMMER PROGRAM

LESSONS: TENNIS, SWIMMING, WATERSKIING.

CANOE TRIPS: DAY TRIPS AND OVERNIGHT.

Next week: Three-day canoe trip. Ages 10–16.
Limited space. Sign up now!

To find out more, visit or call the Bailey Bay Inn.

"Wow," said Mel. "Mr. Magee is really going all out!" Mr. Magee was the new owner of the Bailey Bay Inn. The Inn had been closed for over twenty years. This summer, Mr. Magee bought the place and fixed it up. The Inn had reopened just last week.

"The summer program is a good idea," said Diana. "It will help parents who are staying at the Inn. They can keep their kids busy. Plus Mr. Magee will make more money. He can sell to guests at his hotel *and* people from Deer Lake."

Mel raised her eyebrows. Diana's dad was a rich businessman. Clearly, Diana was learning to think like he did.

Suddenly, Mel heard a voice say, "I see you found my flyer."

The three girls looked up at the same time. The cute guy was standing right there.

"Oh, um, hi," said Mel.

"Hi there," Diana said smoothly. "We were just checking out your program."

"Great!" said the guy. He smiled at the girls. "I hope you'll sign up for something."

"We just might," Diana said. She looked up at him through her eyelashes.

Allison choked on her milk shake.

"Well, I'm Jake Magee. My uncle owns the Bailey Bay Inn. I'll be working there for the rest of the summer."

"I'm Mel Randall," said Mel. "This is Allison Suwan and Diana Standing."

"What do you do at the Inn?" Allison asked.

"My first job is to go on the three-day canoe trip," Jake said. "I'm one of the trip leaders."

Diana leaned forward. "Isn't that funny?" she said. "We were just talking about going on that trip."

Mel and Allison looked at each other.

Diana shot them a warning look. Then she smiled up at Jake. "Yes," she said quickly. "Canoeing and camping. The three of us do that kind of stuff all the time."

Chapter 2

Allison choked on her milk shake again. Diana pounded her on the back.

"Great!" said Jake. "I guess I'll see you next week, then."

"See you around," said Mel.

Diana waved her fingers at Jake as he walked away.

"Um, Diana? Are you out of your mind?" Allison asked.

"Shhhhh!" whispered Diana. She waited until Jake left the store. Then she turned back to Mel and Allison. "You guys *have* to come on this trip with me," she said.

"No we don't," said Allison.

"Please!" Diana begged. "That guy is really cute. Did you see those blue eyes? Yum."

"You have to be kidding. You're *not* signing up for that trip just to get a guy," said Allison.

"You guys both have boyfriends!" Diana said. "You hang out together. It's not fair. I feel left out. I want a boyfriend, too."

Mel started to feel sorry for her. It was true. Mel spent a lot of time with Will. Allison spent a lot of time with her boyfriend, Kyle Jordan. And the four of them did a lot of stuff together. Without Diana.

"Er, I hate to remind you," Mel said to Diana. "But you *hate* canoeing. And you've never been camping in your life."

"I can fake it," Diana said.

"Jake looks like an outdoorsy type. He'll see right through you," said Allison.

"Not if you guys help me," said Diana. "I'll look like a real camper if you give me tips and cover for me. Then Jake will like me for sure."

Allison shook her head. "I've heard about your ideas on how to get a boyfriend. It will never work."

Diana frowned at Mel. Mel shrugged. Diana had a brother named Ted. Earlier in the summer, he had liked Mel. Diana had tried to set up Mel and Ted. That was before Mel found out that Ted was a jerk. And before she found out that Will was a really great guy. Cute, too.

"It *will* work," said Diana. "Trust me."

Allison looked doubtful.

Mel sighed. "All right, I'll ask my dad if I can go."

Diana leaned across the table. She put her hand on Mel's arm. "Thank you!" Then she looked over at Allison. "Allison, *please* come."

Allison crossed her arms. "I don't think so."

Mel suddenly had a thought. *A canoe trip might be good for them. Allison and Diana would really get to know each other. If they still hate each other afterward, then I'll give up. But I have to give it a shot. Just this one shot.*

Mel turned to Allison. "You do love to go canoeing and camping," she said.

Diana put her hand on Allison's arm. "I really need your help," she said. "I can watch what you do. I'll try to be like you."

"Uh huh," said Allison. "Whatever."

"Jake *has* to see that I'm friends with you two. Then he'll think I'm an outdoor person, just like you guys."

"Yeah, he'll just have to overlook one thing," said Allison. "The fact that you don't actually like being outdoors."

Mel looked at Diana. "You *will* have to swim in the lake, you know." So far this summer, Diana hadn't been in the lake once. She thought the water was gross. She would rather swim in a pool.

Diana paused. Then she took a deep breath. "I can do it. I know I can."

Suddenly, Allison laughed. "It would be pretty funny to watch."

"So you'll come?" Diana asked.

Allison shrugged. "I'll think about it."

"Kyle has to work all next week, anyway," Mel pointed out. "What else will you do?"

"I can think of a bunch of things, actually," said Allison.

"But this will be the most fun thing," Diana said.

"And it might be the funniest," Mel joked.

Allison grinned. "True enough."

Diana and Mel both looked at Allison. They waited.

Finally, Allison threw up her hands. "All right, you win. I'll go."

Chapter 3

The three girls finished their drinks and left Charlie's. They put on their sunglasses. Then they stepped outside into the sun. Downtown Deer Lake was busy. The streets were full of people. Some people were riding bikes. Others were walking their dogs. Parents were walking with kids and babies.

Mel, Allison, and Diana walked home along Skokie Road. It was a long, winding dirt road. There were trees on one side and cottages on the other. The lake was behind the cottages. Mel could hear speedboats zipping around. A warm wind carried the smell of water, sand, and pine trees. It was a perfect summer day.

Before long, they reached Mrs. Bergeron's cottage. Mrs. Bergeron was Will's grandma. Will was staying with her for the summer. His twin cousins were staying there, too.

"Hey," Mel said. "I'm going to stop here and see if Will is home. I'll talk to you later."

The girls said good-bye. Mel watched Diana and Allison walk away. It would take them two minutes to get to Diana's cottage. *I hope they can stay friendly for that long*, Mel thought.

The front door of Mrs. Bergeron's cottage banged shut. Will was standing on the front deck. "Hey," he called.

He looks cute, Mel thought. His short brown hair was wet. "Hi," she said, smiling. "I was just walking by. Did you just go swimming?"

"Yeah," said Will. He smiled and looked down at his feet. Then he looked up at Mel. "Do you, um, want a drink or something?"

"No thanks. I just had a milk shake at Charlie's," Mel said. She took Will's hand. "Let's go sit."

Mel pulled Will over to a big porch swing. It squeaked as they sat down.

"Who did you go to Charlie's with?" Will asked Mel.

"Diana and Allison," Mel replied.

Will raised his eyebrows. "Together?"

Mel nodded. "It's a plan I'm working on. I want to get them to be friends."

"Good luck!" Will said, laughing. "You'll need it, with those two."

"You might be right," Mel said. "Anyway, listen to this. The Bailey Bay Inn has a summer program. They have lessons and canoe trips and stuff."

"Yeah? Where did you see that?" asked Will.

"We met Mr. Magee's nephew today," Mel replied. "Jake. He's working at the Bailey Bay Inn for the summer. He told us about it." She laughed. "Diana has her eye on Jake already."

Will rolled his eyes.

"There's a three-day canoe trip next week. We're going to sign up," Mel said.

"Cool," said Will. "That will be fun. I haven't done a canoe trip since camp last year."

Mel frowned. *Oops. He took that the wrong way. I didn't mean to invite him. Will the girls be mad?* "Oh, um, if you want to come, let me ask the girls, okay?"

Will's cheeks turned red. "Never mind. If you don't want me to come, that's all right."

"It's not that," said Mel. She felt terrible. "It's just that we planned it as a girls' trip. I didn't think you'd *want* to come."

"I like doing stuff with you," said Will quietly. He stared at the ground.

"And I like doing stuff with you," Mel told him. "I do want you to come on the canoe trip. Really. I just didn't think you'd want to. Forget what I said about asking the girls. Just come."

Will shrugged.

Mel kept talking. "You can find out more about it at the Inn. I'm going to talk to my dad later. Then I'll go to the Inn and sign up tomorrow. Maybe we can sign up together."

Will gave Mel a sideways look. "All right," he said. "If you're sure."

"I'm sure!" Mel gave Will a hug. "I'm really sure. You're one of my best friends here."

"I am?" Will leaned back and looked at Mel. He grinned. "Really?" he said.

"Well, you're in the top ten," Mel teased.

Will reached over and started tickling her. Mel screamed and tickled him back. Then, all of a sudden, Will stopped and looked up.

Mel looked up, too. She heard a giggle. *Where is that coming from?*

Will jumped up and ran around to the side of the porch. Two heads popped up near the railing. Two baseball caps went flying. Two boys started running down the path beside the cottage. Will took off after them.

Mel groaned. Benny and Joey were Will's twin cousins. They were eleven years old. *And that explains it all*, thought Mel.

"Sorry about that," Will said when he got back. He was out of breath. "I chased them all the way down to the beach."

"It's okay," Mel said, laughing. "Anyway, I have to get home. I'll see you tomorrow."

"Sure," said Will. He looked at his watch. "My mom is going to call any minute." Will's mom had to work in the city for the summer. She called Will all the time to check up on him.

"Um…" said Will. He looked over his left shoulder. He looked over his right shoulder. Then he leaned in and gave Mel a quick kiss.

Mel heard a loud giggle behind them. Will turned around. Benny and Joey were standing by the deck, pointing.

"Arrrrgh!" Will yelled, running after them again. "Bye, Mel," he called over his shoulder.

Mel waved and walked home.

Chapter 4

The Randalls' cottage was just down the road. Mel found her dad sitting on the back deck. He was working on his laptop computer. Mel's younger sister was there, too. Sara was writing on a pad of paper.

"Hi, Dad," Mel said. She sat down next to her sister. "Hi, Sarabean. What are you doing?"

Sara didn't look up. "I'm writing a story. I'm going to work for a magazine, like Dad." She was writing madly on the page.

Mr. Randall winked at Mel. "We figured she should get an early start."

"Cool," Mel said, smiling. "Do you think the magazine will buy her article?"

Sara stopped writing and looked up at Mel. "Duh! No," she said. "I'm only seven. I'm just practicing."

"Oh, right." Mel looked around for her older sister. "Where's Lindsay? At work?"

"Yes," said Mr. Randall. "And she's having dinner with Ian. So the three of us are on our own tonight."

Ian was Allison's older brother. He was also Lindsay's boyfriend.

"Can I ask you something, Dad?" Mel said. She told him about the Bailey Bay Inn summer program. Then she explained the girls' plan to go on the canoe trip.

"How much does it cost?" her dad asked.

"I don't know," Mel replied.

"Let me call the Inn," Mr. Randall said. "Then we can decide, okay?"

Mel nodded. "Thanks, Dad."

Mr. Randall went inside to make the call. Mel lay down on a deck chair. She stared out at the lake. The sound of a speedboat drifted over from next door. Then the Standings' big boat raced past the Randalls' dock.

Mr. Standing was driving the boat. Ted was behind the boat on a pair of waterskis. He waved at Mel. Then he turned on his skis and sprayed water toward the Randalls' dock.

"Show off!" Mel muttered to herself. The boat sped away across the water.

Mel jumped up as her dad came back outside. "How much is the canoe trip?" she asked him. "Can I go?"

"Well, it's not cheap," Mr. Randall replied.

Mel's heart sank. *So much for the plan to get Diana and Allison to be friends.*

"But, it *is* your last summer to be a kid and have fun," her dad said. The Randall family had a rule. Kids had to get jobs when they turned fifteen. Next summer, Mel would turn fifteen. She would have to get a summer job.

This summer, Mel could hang out with her friends when she wanted to. She did make a bit of pocket money. She made hemp jewelry and sold it at the General Store. She also did some babysitting. But for the most part, her time was her own.

Mel bit her lip and looked at her dad. "So, um, can I go?" she asked.

Mr. Randall nodded. "You can go. Next summer, you may not have the chance to do a trip like this."

"Yes!" Mel threw one fist in the air. Then she ran over and hugged her dad. "Thank you! Thank you! Thank you!"

Her dad smiled down at her. "You can thank your Aunt Clare, too. She sent some money for you girls for the summer."

"Cool!" Mel said. Aunt Clare was her mom's sister. She helped out their family a lot. Mel's mom had died when Mel was young.

Thank you, Aunt Clare, Mel said silently. *Thanks to you, my friendship plan might work out after all!*

Chapter 5

The next day, Mel went to visit Will. She found him fishing off the end of his grandma's dock.

"Hi, Will!" Mel called. She ran across the beach to the dock.

Will looked over his shoulder. "Hey," he said. Then he looked back out at the lake.

"I knocked on your door, but no one answered." Mel kicked off her shoes and sat down beside Will. She lowered her feet into the cool water.

"Yeah, Grandma took the twins into town," Will said.

"Thank goodness," Mel joked.

Will didn't laugh.

"What's wrong?" Mel asked. Will seemed like he was in a bad mood.

He looked at her and forced a smile. "Nothing. I'm just…nothing. Never mind."

Mel gave him a sideways look. "Okay. Are you sure?"

"Yeah."

"Catch anything?" Mel asked.

"No."

Mel decided to tell him the happy news. Maybe that would put him in a good mood. "My dad said I can go on the canoe trip next week," she said. "Do you want to go and sign up with me?"

Will frowned. "No," he said. "I've been thinking about it. I don't really want to go."

"Oh," said Mel. *Yesterday he said he likes hanging out with me. He wanted to go on the trip. Today he doesn't want to go. What is that about?*

"Why don't you stay here next week?" Will asked. "You can hang out with me. We don't need to go on a canoe trip." He started reeling in his fishing line.

Mel stared at him. "I already made a plan with Allison and Diana. I can't back out on them now."

"I don't know why you even want to hang out with Diana. She's a rich snob," Will said.

"She's not that bad!" Mel said. "And besides, she's my neighbor."

Will closed his tackle box and stood up. "Yeah, well, I'm not going," he said. "I'm not spending three days camping with Diana."

Mel stood up, too. "But you'd be spending most of your time with me!"

Will marched down the dock. He carried his fishing rod in one hand. His tackle box was in the other. "I'm not going!" he said loudly.

Mel ran to catch up. She followed Will up the path to the cottage. *What is his problem?* she wondered. *He's acting like he's mad at me.*

Will put his fishing gear under the porch. "Do you want to come in?" he asked Mel gruffly. "We could play cards or something."

Mel put her hands on her hips. "No! I want to go to the Bailey Bay Inn. I have to sign up for the canoe trip. But I guess I'll go by myself."

"Fine," said Will. "See you later." He stomped up the back steps.

"Fine. See you," said Mel. She ran down the driveway to Skokie Road. Then she ran all the way to the Bailey Bay Inn.

Chapter 6

By the time Mel reached the Inn, she was out of breath. Her legs burned from running. The double front doors of the Inn were open. Inside, Jake Magee was sitting behind a small desk. He was reading a book.

"Hi, Jake," Mel called.

Jake looked up. He quickly put his book in a drawer. "Hi," he said.

"I met you the other day at Charlie's," said Mel. "I'm here to sign up for the canoe trip."

"Oh, yeah," said Jake. "Your friend was already here."

"Who? Allison?" Mel asked.

"No, your other friend. Diana."

"Diana, right," said Mel. *I should have guessed,* she thought to herself.

Jake pulled out a pad of paper. He added Mel to the list of names. Mel paid him with a check from her dad.

"So I hear that you girls have done a lot of canoeing," Jake said.

"Oh, er...yes," said Mel. That wasn't a lie, if by "you girls" he meant Mel and Allison.

"I can't believe you did a two-week trip. That's pretty cool," Jake said.

Mel laughed nervously. *What did Diana tell this guy?* "Yeah, well, I like canoeing," she told him. That was true. And she *had* done a two-week trip. Just not this summer. And it was with her dad, not her friends. She looked over her shoulder at the front door. *Get me out of here!* she thought.

"Well, it's great that you girls know what you're doing," Jake said. "You can help me with the other kids."

"Um, right. Sure," Mel said.

"Okay, you're all signed up," Jake said. He handed her a few pieces of paper. "There's a list of stuff you'll need to bring. Oh, and your dad has to sign this consent form."

"Great, thanks!" said Mel.

"No problem," Jake replied. "I'll see you next week."

"See you!" Mel walked quickly to the front door. She had almost made it when Jake called her name. She turned around.

"Hey," he said. "Um, does your friend Diana—" The phone rang. He and Mel both looked at it. "Never mind." Jake picked up the phone. "Good morning. Bailey Bay Inn," he said. He waved one hand at Mel.

Mel waved back and made her escape. *Phew! That was close!* she thought. *I wonder what Jake was going to ask about Diana. And I wonder what Diana told Jake earlier.*

She walked back down Skokie Road. It was time to pay Diana a visit.

Mrs. Standing answered the door when Mel knocked. She sent Mel upstairs.

Mel stopped when she saw Diana's room. "What the...?" Stuff was lying all over the place. A brand new arctic sleeping bag. A small tent. A fancy backpack. Hiking boots. A fishing hat. Clothes. The floor and bed were covered.

Diana was sitting on the floor. "Mel, I'm so glad you're here," she said. "I need help."

"What is all this stuff?" Mel asked.

"My gear," Diana replied. "I went shopping this morning."

Mel's mouth fell open. "This stuff is all *new?*" she asked. *This must have cost a fortune!*

"Yes, well, I didn't have any camping gear," Diana said with a shrug.

"But...but..." said Mel. "The Bailey Bay Inn will give us most of the stuff we need. Didn't you get a list when you signed up?"

"Yes," Diana said. "But won't it look better if I have my own gear?"

"No!" said Mel. "Not if you can totally tell that it's all brand new!"

"Oh." Diana frowned. Then she smiled at Mel. "You see? This is why I need your help."

"Uh huh," said Mel.

"You can help me sort through things." Diana patted the tent. "And you can help me practice setting up the tent. We can go out in the front yard."

"Okay, I guess," Mel said. *Allison will laugh her head off when she hears about this.*

"Oh, and I signed up for a first aid course," Diana added. "It's this weekend. My dad is driving me into the city for it."

"Um, Diana?" Mel said. "You might be going a little overboard here."

"No way!" said Diana. "I want to learn as much as I can. We leave in less than a week! I *have* to look like I know what I'm doing. Jake thinks I go canoeing all the time. He thinks I've done a two-week canoe trip!"

"I know," Mel said. She shot Diana a dark look. "I can't believe you told him that."

Diana just smiled. "I have to go to the city anyway. I have to buy a few more things."

Mel looked at all the stuff piled around the room. "Like what?" she asked.

"Like a battery-powered hair dryer," Diana said. "Do you know, I couldn't find one anywhere in Deer Lake?"

"Um, that's because…" Mel bit her lip to stop herself from laughing. "There's no such thing as a battery-powered hair dryer."

Diana ran one hand through her long hair. "But how do you style your hair?" she asked.

"Um, you let the sun dry it," Mel told her. "Or you just wear a hat." She watched a look of horror appear on Diana's face. *What have I got myself into?* Mel wondered. *Diana is never going to make it through this trip!*

Chapter 7

A few days later, Mel was packing her bag. *Why hasn't Will called?* she wondered. *He knows I'm going on this trip tomorrow. It's like he's avoiding me. Maybe he doesn't want to hang out with me anymore. Should I call him?* She stuffed a pair of socks into her pack. *No! HE is the one that was in a bad mood.*

Mel really began to look forward to her trip. Out in the woods, she wouldn't have to think about Will. It would just be Mel, the canoe, and the open lake. Well, Allison would be there, too. And Diana. And a bunch of other kids and two leaders.

Suddenly, the phone rang.

"*Melllllllllll!*" her sister Lindsay called. "Phone for you! It's *Willlllll!*"

Mel picked up the phone. "Hi, Will!" she said cheerfully. She decided to act like nothing was wrong. Maybe nothing *was* wrong. Maybe she was just imagining things.

"Hey," said Will.

"What's up?" Mel asked.

"Um, nothing. I just called to…uh…say hi."

"Oh. Hi," said Mel. *And?*

"I wanted to say…you know. I hope you have a good trip."

"Thanks," Mel said. *Even though he sounds like he doesn't mean it.*

"I'm sorry I'm not coming with you," Will said quietly. His voice sounded strange.

"Well, I'll see you when I get back, I guess."

"Okay," said Will.

I'll give him one last chance, Mel thought. "You could come and see us off," she said. "We leave from the public dock in the morning."

"Oh, I…uh…I can't," said Will. "I have to…um…do something with my grandma."

You are such a bad liar, Mel thought angrily. "Fine," she said to Will. "Whatever. I'll see you in a few days." She banged down the phone.

Mel went out to the back deck. The leaves in the trees rustled overhead. Waves slapped against the dock. The sky was completely gray.

Will is acting weird, Mel thought. She was feeling sorry for herself. *Maybe he wants to break up with me. I'll bet he's too chicken to do it. That's why he's been avoiding me lately.*

A few drops of rain fell on the deck. Mel decided to visit Diana. *She should be home from the city by now,* she thought. *She might want more practice setting up her tent.*

Diana was happy to see Mel. "I learned lots of stuff at the first aid course! Now, if anyone breaks a leg, I'll know what to do! That will look good to Jake for sure." She eyed Mel's leg.

Mel put her hands on her hips. "Don't even think about it. I'm not going to break my leg just to help you with Jake."

Diana waved one hand in the air. "Oh, don't worry. I would never ask you to do that."

"I was *kidding*," Mel told her.

"Oh," Diana said. "Anyway, I've done what you told me to do. I've worn my hiking boots for four days straight. Now they don't look so new." She lowered her voice to a whisper. "I even rubbed them in the dirt."

Mel nodded. "Good."

"My parents think I'm nuts," Diana said. She looked a little sad. "They think I won't go through with the trip. They think I can't do it."

"What!" Mel said. "Of course you can do it! What do your parents know?"

Diana shrugged. "I have to finish packing." She looked at all her gear. "Okay, I won't bring my camping stove. Or my new set of camping dishes." She sighed. "They're so cute though. The little pots all fit together. And they're blue! My favorite color."

Mel looked at the pile of clothes on Diana's bed. "You still have way too many clothes," she told her. "You need to cut this pile in half."

"I'm working on it." Diana picked up a bathing suit. She paused. Then she put it away.

Mel pointed to a small pile of bathing suits. "How many bathing suits do you have there?"

"Four," Diana said.

"You only need one," Mel pointed out.

"Okay, three." Diana put away another bathing suit. "They hardly take up any room." She picked up her backpack. "Besides, that's why I bought an extra-big pack. It can hold lots of stuff."

"I should lend you a smaller backpack," said Mel. "We have extra ones at our place."

"I like this one!" said Diana. "Look, it has all kinds of pockets."

"Yeah, but it will be so heavy! You'll hardly be able to carry it!" Mel said.

Diana's mouth fell open. "Wh—what do you mean, *carry it?*"

Mel shot Diana a look. "How do you think your pack will get from one place to another?"

Diana suddenly sat down on her bed. "I thought…" She took a deep breath. "I have to carry my own bag?" she asked in a small voice.

"Of course!" Mel said. "Who did you think would carry it?"

"I don't know!" Diana cried. "Mel, I can't do this. I can't go. I don't know what I was thinking. I'm not the camping type."

Mel sat down beside Diana. "Take a deep breath. Don't panic. Of course you can do it! Think about Jake. Think about me and Allison. We want you to come!"

Diana gave a shaky laugh. "Allison doesn't."

"Well, *I* want you to come," said Mel. "I want you and Allison to get to know each other better. I know you two could be friends. And it's a great chance to get to know Jake. You never know what could happen." She stood up and walked to the door. "Hang on. I'm going to get you a better pack."

Mel ran home and found a smaller backpack for Diana. It looked well used, too.

She brought it back and gave it to Diana. "Here you go!" she said. "Bring as much stuff as you want. It just has to fit in this bag. And you have to be able to lift it. By yourself."

Diana eyed the backpack. "Oh, okay," she said with a sigh.

"I was hoping that we could take the canoe out today." Mel looked out the window. "But it's pouring rain now. I'll just have to teach you on the trip. Don't worry. Canoeing is easy once you get the hang of it."

"If you say so," Diana said, frowning.

"Come to my place tomorrow morning," said Mel. "My dad can drive us down to the public dock."

"Aye, aye, Captain Randall!" Diana joked.

Mel walked home through the rain. *Captain Randall*, she thought. *I like the sound of that.*

Chapter 8

The next morning, the sky was clear and sunny. At nine, Diana knocked on the Randalls' door. Mel waved her into the kitchen.

Diana wore freshly ironed tan shorts and a light blue T-shirt. The colors matched her hiking boots. Her hair hung long and loose. Not one lock was out of place. Mel saw that her nails were cut shorter and painted pale pink.

"I went for the natural look," Diana said. She twirled around. "What do you think?"

"Not bad," Mel said. She looked down at Diana's backpack. It was stuffed full. A hat and a pair of sports sandals were tied to the outside. "Pretty good, actually," she added.

Mr. Randall drove the two girls to the public dock. A bunch of kids were already there. Jake was checking things on a list. Four yellow canoes sat upside down on the dock. Life jackets and paddles were piled nearby.

"Look at Jake," Diana whispered. "Isn't he so cute?" She sighed. Then she looked around the dock. "Hey," she said unhappily. "All the other kids are boys. *Little* boys."

Mel counted five boys. They all looked about ten or eleven years old. Benny and Joey's age. "Oh, man! Little boys can be such a pain," she groaned.

"Tell me about it," said Diana.

"Wait a minute," Mel said. She tapped her chin. "This could actually be a good thing."

"Really? How?" Diana looked doubtful.

"Well, Jake is around sixteen. He'll look after the little kids because it's his job. But in his free time, he'll want to hang out with us. We'll be the oldest ones there."

"Oh, good point," said Diana. She watched Jake out of the corner of her eye. She crossed her arms and smiled. "Mmmm hmmm."

A green car drove up. Allison hopped out. She was carrying a small backpack and a canoe paddle. She ran down to greet Mel and Diana. The girls said hello. Then no one said anything.

Finally, Diana spoke. "That's a really nice paddle," she said. It had elephants painted on it. The elephants were painted in an Asian style. Allison's dad was from Thailand.

"Thanks," said Allison, smiling.

"She painted it herself," Mel said.

Diana looked surprised. "No way!" she said, staring at Allison's paddle. "That's so pretty. Have you done any more?"

Allison shook her head. "No. Why?"

"Well, you could paint paddles and sell them. You could make a lot of money," Diana said. "Most people have plain paddles. How boring is *that*? I bet lots of people would buy yours. They would be cool and different."

"I don't know," Allison said. "I'm not really that good at painting."

"Are you kidding?" Diana pointed to Allison's paddle. "That's great! I love it."

Allison gave Diana a shy smile. "Thanks."

All right! Mel thought to herself. *Allison and Diana are getting along.*

Just then, Jake's voice boomed out over the dock. "Okay, people!" he said. "Over here!"

The group gathered around him. Jake looked up and smiled at the girls. "Hi, everyone," he said. "I'm Jake. I'm one of the trip leaders. The other leader is Mrs. Hill. She's on her way here with our food supplies."

He called each camper's name. Eight kids had signed up for the trip. Jake explained the route they were going to take. Then he went over some safety rules.

After that, he led the group to the canoes. "Take your packs with you in your canoes," he told them. "Two of the canoes will carry three people. The other two boats will carry two people. They will take the camping gear, too."

Jake checked his list. "Let me see. How will this work?" He looked up at the campers. "Okay. Allison and Omar, you go in one canoe. Mel and Gordie, you can take another canoe."

Diana poked Mel in the ribs. "I have to go with you," she whispered.

"Patrick and Tetsuo, you will go with Mrs. Hill," Jake said. "Mike and Diana, you come with me. Now, everyone take a life jacket. Make sure you have a paddle, too."

Diana raised her hand. "Excuse me, Jake!" she called. Then she ran over to him.

When she came back, she had a big smile on her face. "I asked if I could trade canoes," she said. "I'm with you now, Mel."

"Why?" Allison asked. "You had a perfect setup. You were in the same boat as Jake."

"I know," Diana said. "But I couldn't go with him on the first day."

"Is this one of your silly games?" Allison asked coldly. "Pretending you don't like him? Because if it is, I think that's really dumb."

"Nooooo!" Diana said. "I *want* to go with him, but I can't. I have to learn how to canoe first. Mel was going to teach me last week. But we didn't have time."

"Oh," said Allison. "Okay."

Diana picked up a paddle and stared at it. "What if I can't do this?" she whispered to Mel.

"You can do it," Mel told her. "Just stick with me."

Just then, Mrs. Hill drove up in a van. Jake helped her unload a pile of bags.

It took a while to get things ready. Canoes in the water. Gear loaded and tied in. Life jackets on. Kids in their boats.

Finally, the group set off across the lake.

Chapter 9

Mel tightened the ties on her life jacket. She settled in her seat at the back of the canoe. Her knees rested on the bottom of the boat. She put an extra life jacket under them. Otherwise her knees would hurt by the end of the day. Mel guided the canoe with easy strokes. The other boats were ahead of her.

A pile of camping gear sat in the middle of her canoe. Diana sat at the front. Mel watched her struggle with the paddle. "Move your bottom hand down a bit," Mel called quietly.

Diana moved her hand.

"Put your shoulders into it a bit more," Mel added. "There you go. You're doing fine."

Diana looked over her shoulder. She grinned at Mel. "This isn't so bad!" she called back. Then she pulled her paddle too close to the canoe. Her hand bumped against the side of the boat. "Owwww!" she cried. She stopped paddling and shook her fingers.

"Careful!" Mel said.

Diana flipped her long hair over her shoulder. Then she went back to paddling.

The canoes moved across the water. Jake was leading them around the edge of the lake. Soon, they would pass by the Bergeron cottage.

Mel shaded her eyes and peered toward the shore. Two small figures were running down the Bergeron dock. *Must be the twins,* Mel thought. Benny and Joey ran right off the end of the dock. They landed in the lake with a splash.

Will's grandma was sitting on a chair on the beach. She was wearing a big straw hat. When the canoes got close, she stood up. She took off her hat and waved it wildly.

Mel waved back. Will was nowhere to be seen. That made her feel a bit lonely.

Moments later, the canoes passed by the Randall cottage. Mr. Randall, Sara, Lindsay, and Ian were standing on the dock.

Mr. Randall waved.

"Wooooo hooooo!" yelled Lindsay.

Ian whistled.

"Hello, Melonhead!" shouted Sara. She jumped up and down. "Hi, Allison! Hi, Diana!"

Mel put down her paddle and waved.

Diana laughed and waved. All the kids in the other canoes waved, too. That was one thing that Mel liked about Deer Lake. People waved when you passed by in a boat. You didn't have to know the people. They waved anyway. It was just a friendly cottage thing.

Next, they passed by the Standings' dock. No one was in sight. As they paddled on, they saw only trees lining the shore. They would soon be at the end of Deer Lake. A small beach marked the spot where they would stop. Mel had canoed this way many times.

Mrs. Hill's canoe was the first to reach the end of the lake. She and the boys climbed out onto the shore. Mel called a warning to Diana. "We're going to have to portage now."

Diana looked over her shoulder at Mel. "What does that mean?" she asked.

"It means we carry our canoes to the next lake," Mel said. "But don't worry. These canoes are pretty light. Stop paddling for a second. Watch what those guys are doing."

Their canoe slowed down. Mel and Diana watched what was happening up ahead. The other two canoes pulled up to the shore. Jake led the five boys along a path into the woods. Mrs. Hill picked up a canoe all by herself. She lifted it over her head. Then she followed the boys into the woods.

Diana looked back at Mel and frowned. "I don't think I can do that," she said.

"You don't have to do it by yourself," said Mel. "We'll do it together."

"Maybe Jake would carry it for us," Diana said. They were getting close to the shore.

"Maybe he would," Mel said. "But this is your big chance! You can show him that you know what you're doing."

Diana frowned. "I guess," she said.

Mel was surprised. Usually Diana was more sure of herself. Now she seemed to think she couldn't do anything. *I hope she snaps out of it*, thought Mel. *Because it's show time!*

"Here we go!" she called to Diana. The front of their canoe hit the sand.

Chapter 10

Diana looked back at Mel with a worried look on her face.

Allison ran over to meet them. "Jump out, Diana. I'll help you pull up your canoe."

Diana looked around and then jumped out. She landed in a few inches of water. "Ahhh!" she cried. She looked down at her wet boots.

Allison took Diana's arm and pulled her out of the way. Then she dragged the canoe farther onto the beach. Mel hopped out onto the sand.

"Are you girls okay?" Jake called. He was coming back out of the trees.

"Fine!" called Diana, waving.

"Yeah, no problem," Allison said. "We'll bring this canoe over."

"Great," said Jake. He picked up one of the other canoes. He lifted it over his head. Then he carried it along the path.

"My feet are wet," Diana complained.

"Live with it," said Allison. "You can change into your sandals later. Now, help me with the gear."

The three girls took the camping gear out of the canoe. They piled the bags on the beach. Mrs. Hill appeared with the troop of boys. They each picked up one bag. Then they marched back along the path through the forest.

"Okay, let's get this canoe," said Mel. She put on her backpack. Then she stood at the back of the canoe.

Allison stood at the front, on the same side. "One, two, three!" she counted. She and Mel lifted the canoe. They rested it on their thighs. "One, two, three!" Allison counted again. They rolled the canoe over and lifted it in the air. They held it upside down over their heads.

"Okay!" Mel called. She let the sides of the canoe rest on her shoulders. Her head was inside the boat now.

Allison called Diana over. "Come and take the front."

Diana moved into Allison's spot. Allison helped Diana get a firm hold on the canoe.

"I can't see!" Diana said, with the canoe over her head.

Allison laughed. She took the front of the canoe and lifted it. "Here. Move up a little," she told her. Diana moved up. Allison lowered the canoe. Now it was resting on Diana's left shoulder. Her head was clear.

"Hold the other side with your left hand," Allison said. "That's it." She let go of the canoe. When she was sure Diana was steady, Allison backed away.

"Now what?" Diana asked.

Allison picked up a couple of bags. "Now you follow me," she said.

Diana and Mel started to walk. They followed Allison along the path. It took a minute to get used to walking with the canoe.

"Piece of cake, huh, Diana?" Mel said.

"Um, *no*. How far do we have to go?" Diana asked. She was puffing a bit.

"It's just a few minutes," Allison said. "You're lucky. This is a pretty short portage."

Jake passed them on the path. He was going the other way. "Looking good, girls!"

Diana's head turned as she watched Jake walk by. She nearly ran into a bush.

"Eyes front!" Allison hissed.

The path ended at another beach. Mrs. Hill greeted the girls as they put down the canoe. "We're just having a snack break," she told them. "There are drinks and granola bars in that bag. Help yourselves."

The girls stood on the sand. They looked out at the lake in front of them.

"It's so quiet here," Diana said.

All of a sudden, two boys burst out of the bushes. They ran across the beach, yelling their heads off. Gordie ran out behind them. He tagged Omar, who was standing on the beach. "You're it!" he shouted. Omar spun around. Then he took off after the other boys.

The girls looked at each other and started laughing. "So much for quiet," said Mel.

"Hey, what do I do when I have to pee?" Diana whispered. "Will there be a washroom?"

Mel waved her hand at the forest. "You go in the woods," she said.

Diana stared at her in shock.

"Haven't you ever peed in the woods before?" asked Allison.

"Of course not!" Diana snapped. "Why would I pee in the woods? I use a washroom like a regular person."

Allison grinned and pointed to the trees. "Go on," she said.

"What if somebody sees me?" Diana asked. Her voice squeaked.

"We'll keep a lookout," said Mel. "You need to go way into the woods, anyway. You can't pee too close to the lake or the path. Try over there, through those big bushes."

"Don't pee on your boots," said Allison helpfully. "And you need to pick leaves to use as toilet paper. But don't pick poison ivy."

Diana looked like she was going to cry.

Mel frowned at Allison. "Stop that." She pulled a plastic bag out of her backpack. It had a roll of toilet paper in it. "You don't have to use leaves for toilet paper," she told Diana. She handed her the bag. "But you have to bury the toilet paper you use."

Diana took the toilet paper. She pressed her lips together. Then she carefully picked her way into the trees.

Chapter 11

"You were right," said Allison. "This trip is going to be a lot of fun."

Mel wagged her finger at her friend. "Be nice," she said. "She's really trying."

"I know," said Allison.

A few minutes later, Diana came running out of the trees. The toilet paper was tucked under her arm. "I did it!" she said when she reached them.

"Good for you," said Mel.

Diana shivered. "I don't really want to have to do it again, though."

"Well, I think you'll have to," said Allison. "Unless you can hold it for the next two days."

Diana closed her eyes and sighed. Then she ran to wash her hands in the lake.

"Okay, folks! Over here!" Mrs. Hill called. "We're about to canoe down Crow Lake. This is a conservation area. That means that the trees and plants and animals are protected here. That's why you don't see any cottages on this lake. And you won't see any speedboats.

"We'll stop for lunch at Turtle Island. You can have a swim after lunch. Then we'll get back in the canoes. We're going to paddle to the end of Crow Lake. That's where we'll set up camp for the night. Are you ready to go?"

"Yeah!" shouted the boys. They ran for the canoes.

"Hold on!" Jake called after them. "Take a bag with you." The boys ran back. They helped load the gear back into the canoes.

Diana sat down and took off her boots and socks. She put on her sports sandals. "Ahhh, much better," she said. She stood up and took a few steps along the beach. Then she frowned and stamped one foot. "I have sand between my toes," she complained. "I hate that."

Mrs. Hill walked around with a bottle of sunblock. She made sure the boys were well covered with it. "Hats and life jackets!" she shouted. "I want to see you all wearing them!"

"I've got sunblock," said Diana. She pulled a bottle out of her pack. She offered it to Mel and Allison. "It's made for your face. It won't give you zits."

"Oh, thank goodness," said Allison, rolling her eyes. But she smiled and took the sunblock.

Soon, the canoes were on their way. Crow Lake was much quieter than Deer Lake. Not another boat was in sight.

"Pssst, Diana!" Mel whispered. "Look!" She pointed at a great blue heron. It was sitting on the shore. All of a sudden, the huge bird took flight. The girls stopped paddling. They watched the heron fly across the lake.

"Wow!" said Diana.

The heron flew into a small bay. It landed on a rock and folded its great wings.

Their canoe had drifted behind the others. Jake turned around to look for them. Mel waved. "Let's catch up," she said.

Diana picked up her paddle. "Let's pass them!" she said.

The two girls started paddling hard. They soon reached Jake's canoe. Mike and Gordie were sitting in front of Jake. The two young boys were paddling lightly. At one point, Mike dropped his paddle in the water. Gordie hit the water with his paddle and splashed Mike.

"Cool it, guys!" Jake called. He leaned over the side and snagged Mike's paddle. Mel thought she saw him smile at Diana, but she wasn't sure.

Mel and Diana passed the boys' canoe. "Hold onto your paddles," Mel warned Mike and Gordie. "See that narrow spot up ahead? The current gets a bit stronger there."

The girls pulled far ahead. Diana was paddling hard. "Don't worry. You look good," Mel called to Diana. "I'm sure Jake noticed."

Diana looked back at Mel. "It's not that. I don't want Jake to see us go through the hard part. In case I screw up, you know?"

"You won't screw up," Mel told her. "Just pay attention and do what I tell you."

They reached the narrow end of the bay. The water flowed quickly here. In some places, rocks were sticking out of the water. It was too late to turn back. The canoe was pulled along by the strong current.

Chapter 12

Large rocks towered up on either side of them. It was a very narrow spot. Mel paddled with all her strength. She had to keep them on course. She guided the canoe around the rocks.

"Paddle harder!" she yelled at one point. Diana paddled like mad. The canoe swooped past a huge rocky island. Then Mel yelled, "Change sides!" Diana paddled on the other side of the canoe.

At last, they reached an open area where the water was calm. Diana's hands were white. She was holding her paddle tightly.

"You can rest now!" Mel called to her. "You did it!"

Diana laid her paddle across the sides of the canoe. She shook her fingers. Then she smiled back at Mel. "Yeah, I did it!"

Mel pointed to a tiny island. "That's Turtle Island." Two yellow canoes sat on the shore. She could see boys jumping across the rocks.

Diana and Mel paddled to the island. Mel's stomach was rumbling. She could hardly wait for lunch. Jake's canoe arrived, and then the group ate. They ate a pile of sandwiches in record time.

After lunch, Gordie and Omar went around with a plastic bag. They collected all the trash. Jake told them that it was important not to leave trash in natural areas. It all had to be carried back home in the canoes.

Then Jake and Mrs. Hill took the boys swimming. "Make sure you keep your life jackets on!" Jake told them. "The current is strong here."

"Wear your sports sandals in the water, too," added Mrs. Hill. "I don't want anyone to hurt their feet."

"I can't wait to get in the water!" Allison said. She pulled off her T-shirt and shorts. She wore a blue bathing suit under her clothes.

"Me neither!" said Mel. "I need to cool off." She saw that Diana wasn't getting ready to swim. "Are you coming, Diana? Great time to show off your bathing suit." She wiggled her eyebrows and nodded at Jake.

Allison rolled her eyes.

"No...I don't want to," Diana said, eyeing the water.

"Are you chicken?" asked Allison.

"Allison!" Mel said. Then she turned to Diana. "It's totally safe, Diana. The water is not dirty. Come swimming with us."

"I'll go next time," said Diana.

Allison shook her head. "Whatever." She put on her life jacket and slid into the water.

Mel shrugged at Diana. "Next time, then," she said.

The lake was nice and cool. Mel swam around a bit. Then she floated on her back and looked up at the sky. The sound of boys shouting and splashing drifted through the air.

Mel looked over at Turtle Island. Diana was sitting on a big rock. She had one foot in the water.

Well, that's a start, Mel thought. She climbed out of the lake and sat beside Diana. It was a shady spot, but the rock was warm. Mel's bathing suit was dry in minutes. She lay back on the rock and closed her eyes.

She may have fallen asleep. The sound of a loud whistle was the next thing she heard. "Time to go!" Mrs. Hill called.

Mel and Diana walked over to the canoes. Allison and Mrs. Hill were packing up gear. The boys were putting on sunblock.

"We have one more hour of paddling," Jake announced. "Then we'll set up camp."

They set out across the lake again. The far end of Crow Lake was open and calm. Mel loved the feel of paddling. She loved the feel of her back and arms moving. She loved to feel the sun on her face.

I haven't thought about Will all day, Mel realized. Of course, that made her start thinking about him. *I wish he were here. I like canoeing with him. We've had some fun times. Even the time we got lost. What if he doesn't want to be my boyfriend anymore? What if he doesn't even want to be friends? I'll be really…what?* Mel wasn't sure how she would feel. *I'll be upset. I'll be angry.* She sighed. *I'll be sad.*

Chapter 13

Jake led the group after lunch. It took an hour to reach the end of Crow Lake. They unloaded the canoes on the shore. Then Mrs. Hill led them to a nearby clearing. It was a well-used camping spot. There was even a blackened fire pit. It had a grate for cooking.

Everyone lugged the gear up from the shore. Mrs. Hill pointed out places where they could set up tents. Jake put a tent bag in each spot. Then he turned to the campers. "Let's see if any of you can set up a tent!"

Mike and Omar ran over to one of the spots. Omar emptied the tent bag. Mike started laying out the pieces.

"I'll do one!" Diana said quickly. She flipped her hair and smiled at Jake. Then she ran over to one of the other tents. Jake smiled and watched her go.

Mrs. Hill set up a small tent for herself.

Mel walked over to see if Diana was okay. "Do you need any help?" she asked quietly.

Diana was trying to fit two poles together. "Yes. Stupid…pole…things. This isn't the same as the one I practiced on at home."

Together, the two girls put up the yellow tent. "Hey, Diana," Mel whispered. "Jake is setting up the cooking stuff. Why don't you run over and see if he needs help?"

"Okay!" Diana ran her fingers through her hair. "How do I look?"

"Good. Go!" Mel shooed Diana away.

In a few seconds, she was back. "He doesn't want help," Diana said unhappily. "Or maybe he was just trying to get rid of me."

Mel looked over at Jake. He was sitting by himself, taking things out of bags. "I'm sure that's not it. Maybe he just wants some time alone. He *was* trapped in a boat with two bratty boys all day."

Diana sighed. "Maybe."

"Let's go for a walk," Mel said. *That will take Diana's mind off Jake.* "I can show you what poison ivy looks like. Then you won't step in any by mistake."

"Good idea," Diana said. Allison joined them. The three girls started off into the woods.

The first thing they found was Mrs. Hill. She was hanging a sheet between two trees. "I'm setting up a bathroom," she told them.

Diana clapped her hands. "Thank you!"

"Use this if you have to pee," said Mrs. Hill. "If you have to…ahem…do anything else, use the outhouse. It's not far. Just follow that path there." She pointed at a path running through the trees. Then she headed back to camp.

"I hate this," sighed Diana. "I have to pee right now. I think I'll use the outhouse."

"Trust me on this one," said Mel. "You don't want to use the outhouse. Not unless you *really* have to."

"Oh, go on," said Allison. "Use the outhouse. We'll wait right here."

Diana looked from Mel to Allison. Then she turned and ran down the path to the outhouse.

She was back in less than a minute. She was holding her nose. "Very funny, Allison. I think

I'll use this bathroom." Diana walked behind the sheet hanging from the trees. "Hey!" she yelled. "This isn't a bathroom. What was Mrs. Hill talking about?"

Mel looked behind the sheet. She saw an area of bare ground. She also saw a small shovel sticking out of the dirt. "Just dig a little hole," she told Diana. "Pee in the hole. Then cover it with dirt when you're done."

Diana let out a choked sound. "Oh," she said weakly.

The girls each took a turn in the bathroom. Then they went back to camp. Mrs. Hill was setting out sleeping pads and sleeping bags. Patrick was putting them in the tents. Tetsuo and Omar were playing a Game Boy. Jake was watching Mike build a fire in the fire pit.

The girls went over to the fire. "That's good," Jake was saying. "You just need smaller sticks." He looked up at the girls. "Hi," he said.

"Hi," said Allison. "What's for dinner?"

"Hot dogs, I think," said Jake. "I'll go check with Mrs. Hill. Diana, can you help Mike light the fire?"

"No problem," said Diana. After Jake left, she walked over to Mike. She stared at his pile of sticks. Then she looked helplessly at Allison. "Er, can you...?" She pointed at Mike.

Allison sat down with Mike and helped him with the matches.

Diana sat on a log near the fire pit. Mel sat down beside her. Diana whispered, "See? Did you see how fast Jake took off? I think he's trying to avoid me."

Allison looked up. "Then he's perfect for you," she whispered. "A guy who likes to play games, too!"

"I think Will is playing games," Mel said.

"What?" Diana said.

"What are you talking about?" Allison asked Mel. She sent Mike off to find more wood for the fire.

"It all started when I told him about our trip," Mel said. "Will was upset that I didn't ask him to come. So I asked him to come. Then he said he didn't want to. He was acting like he was mad at me. He hardly talked to me at all last week."

"Maybe he was just busy," said Allison. "That could be why he didn't talk to you."

Mel sighed unhappily. "I think he might want to, you know, break up with me."

Diana put her arm around Mel's shoulders. "No. I don't believe it. Not nice, cute Will."

"I don't believe it either, Mel," said Allison. "I mean, he loves hanging out with you."

"Whatever. I don't know," Mel said. "Forget I said anything. This is supposed to be a girls' trip."

"Yeah," said Allison. Then she winked at Diana. "Except for five little boys and one cute trip leader."

"One *verrrry* cute trip leader," Diana said. "You guys *have* to help me out. What am I doing wrong? Is it the outdoors thing? Can you totally tell that I don't know what I'm doing?"

Allison shook her head. "Actually, you're doing okay. You did really well in the canoe. I think you're a natural."

"Really?" Diana said. "It's not as horrible as I thought it would be. Well, not quite."

"I'm sure Jake thinks you're great," said Mel. "Maybe he's just the silent type."

"Maybe he's shy," said Allison.

"Maybe he has a girlfriend already," Diana said. She frowned.

"Well," said Mel, "there's only one way to find out!"

Chapter 14

Diana narrowed her eyes. "How?" she asked.

"We'll just ask him!" Mel answered.

"Don't you dare," said Diana. "He'll know you're asking for me. Don't do it." She looked at Mel and Allison. They were both grinning. "I'm begging you. Don't do it!"

"Shhhh," hissed Allison. "Here he comes."

Jake was walking back toward the camp-fire. He was carrying a big pot of water. "Where's Mike?" he asked when he got closer.

"Getting more wood," Allison said. "He built a pretty good fire here."

"Great," said Jake. He put the pot on the grate over the fire. Then he sat down on a nearby log. The fire was making crackling and popping sounds. "That *is* a good fire," Jake said. "Mike's a good little camper."

"How was he at canoeing?" Mel asked.

Jake smiled. "Not bad," he said. "But both my guys were tired by the end of the day. I think I did all the paddling toward the end. Good thing we're not doing a longer trip." He rubbed his arm. "We'll trade tomorrow. I'll stick one of you girls with Mike and Gordie."

Diana looked up when Jake said that. *I'll bet she's planning to get in his canoe*, Mel thought.

"Hey, Jake," Allison said suddenly. "Do you have a girlfriend?"

Diana cleared her throat loudly. She glared at Allison.

"No, not right now," Jake said. "Why?"

"Oh, no reason. Never mind," Allison waved one hand. "Mel was just having trouble with her boyfriend. We thought maybe you could give some advice."

It was Mel's turn to glare at Allison. She felt her cheeks turning red.

Allison kept talking to Jake. "But if you don't have a girlfriend..." She shrugged. "Then I guess we can't ask you for advice."

"Well, you could try me," said Jake. "I used to have a girlfriend. I do know *some* stuff." He turned to look at Mel. "What's the trouble?"

Mel felt like grabbing Allison and throwing her in the lake. Instead, she tried to smile at Jake. "Well, my boyfriend was acting weird last week," she said. Then she told him the whole story. How Will seemed angry with her. How he was avoiding her.

Jake looked thoughtful. "Hm," he said. "It does sound like he's upset. But I doubt it's about you. He's just being a guy. Maybe he feels left out. You're spending time with your friends instead of with him."

Mel thought about that. "Then why didn't he just come with us? I asked him to come!"

Jake shrugged. "I don't know. Maybe you should just ask him about it."

"I agree," said Allison. "Take the direct approach. Don't play games." She shot Diana a look. Diana shot a look back.

"Yeah, I guess," Mel said quickly. She didn't want Allison and Diana to start arguing. "Thanks, Jake."

"No problem," he said. "That's what I'm here for." Then he grinned. "Well, kind of." He looked at Diana and Allison. "Anyone else have a question? Anyone else with guy troubles?" he joked.

"Um, no," said Diana.

"Well, we do have one more question," Allison said. She looked at Jake with a cheerful grin. "Diana was wondering how to get a certain guy. You know, how to go about it."

Diana's mouth dropped open. She stared at Allison.

"Allison!" Mel said, trying not to laugh.

"Ah, well, that's no problem," said Jake. He ran one hand through his sandy-colored hair. "Just, er, you know, ask the guy out or something." He seemed uncomfortable. He stared out at the trees over their heads. "Diana shouldn't have any trouble." He stood up and looked at Diana. "Good luck with it." Then he walked away.

The girls watched him disappear down the path to the lake. Diana stood up. "I can't believe you just did that," she said to Allison. Her voice was angry.

"I was just trying to help," Allison said. "See? Now you know that he likes the direct approach. All you have to do is ask him out."

"Yeah, right," said Diana, shaking her head. "I'm sure he guessed that I like him. Did you see how fast he ran out of here? He was afraid that I'd use the direct approach on *him*."

"He wasn't running," said Mel. "Maybe he just had to do something."

"Yeah," said Allison.

"Whatever," Diana said coldly. "Do me a favor, *Allison*. Don't try to give me any more help." She stormed away toward the tents.

Chapter 15

Mel looked at Allison.

Allison looked at Mel. "What?" she said. "What did I do?"

"Can you *please* try to be nice to her?" Mel asked. "Is it really so hard?"

Allison shook her head. "I'm tired of her stupid ideas about guys. I hate girls who play games. Why can't she just be brave and ask him out?"

"Oh, yeah," said Mel. "And you were *so* brave when you met Kyle. *Not.*"

Allison opened her mouth to say something. Then her cheeks turned red. "That was different," she said.

"No it wasn't," said Mel, wagging her finger. "You only *think* you're brave now. But that's because you know Kyle likes you."

"All right, you're right," Allison said. "But I didn't play games. I was just...shy."

"Maybe Diana's shy, too. She just shows it in a different way."

"Yeah, maybe you're right," said Allison.

"So will you stop bugging her?" Mel asked.

"But it's so much fun!" Allison said. Then she sighed. "Oh, okay. I'll stop."

Mrs. Hill came over to the campfire. She called everyone to come for dinner. The five boys came running out of the woods. They started roasting hot dogs over the fire.

Diana came out of her tent and joined the group. She tried to sit by herself. But Mel and Allison moved and sat beside her. Then Jake showed up carrying a few long sticks. He gave one to each of the girls for their hot dogs.

Diana held her hot dog over the fire. She held it a little too close to the flames. The whole thing caught on fire. Diana started shaking her stick. The hot dog fell off and landed in the fire. It curled up in the flames. It quickly turned into a crusty black lump.

Patrick giggled. Then his hot dog fell into the fire, too. The other boys burst out laughing.

"Here," said Allison. "You can have mine." She handed Diana her stick. It had a perfectly roasted hot dog on the end.

Diana took the hot dog. "Thanks," she said.

"I'm sorry," said Allison quietly. "About Jake…and what I said."

Diana smiled a little. "It's okay," she said.

Allison got a fresh hot dog and started roasting. Diana was just staring at her cooked hot dog. Mel handed her a bun.

"I hate hot dogs," Diana said. She took a small bite. Then she leaned over to Mel and Allison. "It's a good thing I brought extra food," she whispered. "I don't think I can eat camping food for three days."

"What did you bring?" asked Allison.

"Peanut butter granola bars," Diana said. "A few chocolate bars. And two small bags of cheese popcorn."

"Yum!" said Allison.

"So *that's* why your backpack is so big," Mel teased.

"Ha ha," Diana said. "No treats for you." She started waving her hand around her head.

"Hey, what's with the bugs all of a sudden? Do they like hot dogs or something?"

"The sun is starting to go down," Allison said. "That's when the mosquitoes come out looking for blood."

"Yeah, but they're only going for my blood. Why aren't they going for yours?" Diana asked. She slapped a mosquito on her neck.

Allison shrugged. "I guess you just smell sweeter," she joked.

Mel leaned over and smelled Diana's hair. "You used scented shampoo to wash your hair. Bugs can smell that stuff from miles away."

"You're kidding me, right?" Diana asked. "What do you guys use to wash your hair?"

"Natural stuff," Allison said. "It doesn't have perfume in it. I have some you can use tomorrow, if you want. It's biodegradable. You can use it in the lake."

"Oh, thanks," groaned Diana. "Now I have to go in the lake."

"You can do it." Mel patted Diana's knee. "We'll go with you."

Diana sighed. Allison got bug spray from Mrs. Hill.

"What's for dessert?" Tetsuo asked.

"Marshmallows!" Jake announced. He held up a huge bag. "Who wants one?"

Right away, all the boys gathered around Jake. Their hands were in the air.

"Like they need *more* sugar," said Allison.

"Boys," Mel said, rolling her eyes.

They all started to roast marshmallows. Diana's caught on fire within seconds. She dropped it and her stick into the fire. She brushed her hands on her legs. "I didn't really want—" she started to say.

Jake leaned over toward her. He handed her the marshmallow he had just roasted.

"Thanks," Diana said shyly.

"No problem," he said. His blue eyes rested on Diana. Then he looked away.

Mrs. Hill started singing camp songs. The group sang along. Jake used a pot for a drum. Allison played the spoons. Mel clapped her hands. The boys picked up whatever they could find and made noise. Diana didn't know any of the songs, but she clapped along.

"We won't have to worry about bears!" Allison shouted. "Not with all this racket!"

Diana's eyes opened wide. "Bears?" she asked. "Did you say *bears?*"

"There are black bears around here," Mel said. "But don't worry. They hardly ever bother people. And look! Mrs. Hill and Jake are putting the food out of reach." She pointed at the two leaders. They were standing beside two large trees. They were far away from the tents and the fire. Mrs. Hill pulled on a rope. Two bags of food rose into the air between the two trees. When they finished, the bags were hanging high off the ground.

"So we're safe," Mel said. "Even if bears smell the food, they won't be able to get it."

"Oh, that's great," said Diana. "So then the bears will just wander around the campsite. They'll be looking for something else to eat. *Like people!*"

"Nah. Bears don't eat people," Mel said.

Allison grinned. "Well, not very often!"

Chapter 16

After that, Diana ran to her tent. She came back carrying her backpack. "Can you help me?" she whispered to Mel. "We should put my pack up the tree, too. I don't want a bear to smell my secret stash of snacks."

Mel slapped her forehead. *I should have thought of that. Diana told us she brought food. It's rule number one when you're camping. No food in the tent!*

"Good thinking," she told Diana.

They took the pack over to Mrs. Hill. Diana got in trouble for bringing her own food. The list of rules had said "NO FOOD." But Mrs. Hill hung Diana's backpack up between the trees.

Before long, it was time for bed. Mrs. Hill took the small tent. Mel, Allison, and Diana shared the yellow tent. The boys argued over who would get to sleep in Jake's tent.

"Poor guy," said Allison. "He has to share a tent with two of the little monsters."

In the end, they tossed a coin. Tetsuo and Gordie got Jake's tent. Omar, Mike, and Patrick shared the fourth tent. Mel heard a lot of giggling coming from the boys' tents. It only lasted a few minutes. Then all was quiet.

The girls talked a little, but they were tired. Allison only teased Diana a bit about Jake. Diana only complained once about sleeping on the ground. Mel fell asleep to the sounds of the forest. The crickets were singing. Frogs were croaking. Once in a while, an owl hooted.

She woke up to the sound of birds chirping. The early morning sun made the walls of the tent glow yellow. Diana and Allison were still asleep. Mel unzipped the tent flap and stepped out. The clearing was empty except for the four quiet tents. Dew covered the grass. She put on her sandals and walked down to the lake. The grass left drops of water on her toes.

The lake was smooth. A light mist hung in the air above the calm water. The sun was starting to burn it off. Mel sat down on a rock. She watched two loons swim across the bay.

When Mel went back to the clearing, Mrs. Hill was up. She had taken all the bags down from the trees. She was setting out food for breakfast. Mel helped Mrs. Hill fill up the water bottles. Jake had boiled water the night before. They used that water to fill the bottles. The lake water was not safe to drink unless it was boiled.

Then Mel ate a bowl of granola. Mrs. Hill sat and ate with her. When they were done, the older woman looked at her watch. "So much for peace and quiet," she said. "It's time to wake everyone up."

"I'll wake up the girls," Mel offered. She took Diana's backpack over to the yellow tent. Allison was already up. She was rolling up her sleeping bag.

Mel crawled over to Diana and shook her shoulder. "Time to get up," she said quietly.

Diana groaned and pulled the sleeping bag over her head. "Too tired," she muttered. "Need more sleep."

Mel yanked on the sleeping bag. "You have to get up *now*," she said. "Or you won't have time to wash your hair."

Diana sat up straight. Then she groaned loudly. "I hurt," she said.

"Where?" Mel asked.

"Everywhere!" Diana raised her arms and then dropped them. "My arms hurt. My back hurts." She looked at her hands. "I'm dirty. And I have blisters."

"Hey, look at it this way," Allison said. "At least you'll get to use your first aid kit. I'll help you with the bandages."

Diana shot her a dark look.

"Just trying to help!" Allison said. "Whatever. You'll feel better after a bath."

"A bath?" said Diana. She rubbed her hands together.

"Well, a bath in the lake," Mel said.

Diana's face fell. "Oh."

Allison opened Diana's backpack. "Here's your towel," she said. She tossed it to Diana. "Geez, you have a lot of stuff in here. What else do you want?"

"I need your shampoo," Diana said. "The lake-friendly stuff."

"Oh, right," said Allison. She handed Diana a bottle.

The girls changed into bathing suits. Then they walked down to the lake. Jake was just coming back to camp. His hair was wet, and he had a towel around his neck. He greeted the girls as they passed by.

When they got down to the water, Diana sighed. "Hello! Did you see how good he looked without a shirt on? I can't believe he saw me with bedhead."

Allison rolled her eyes. Then she splashed into the lake. Mel was right behind her.

Diana got in more slowly. First she sat on a rock and dipped her feet in the water. Then she slid down a little and got her legs wet. Then she slid down a little more. She got wet up to her stomach.

Allison swam over and gave Diana the shampoo. "Just use a little bit," she said.

Diana slowly bent over and got her hair wet. Then she started shampooing.

"See? That's not so bad, is it?" Allison said.

"The water is cold," Diana complained.

Allison groaned. She ignored Diana and went back to swimming.

Mel swam out into the bay. "Swim out here to rinse off!" she called to Diana.

Diana looked over. Her head was covered in suds. She took a deep breath and sank under the water. Then she swam over to Mel. Her long black hair was rinsed clean.

"You did it!" said Mel.

Diana grinned. "Yeah!"

"Let's go!" yelled Allison. She was climbing out of the water.

Mel and Diana swam back to shore. They climbed onto the rocks. Allison handed them their towels.

All of a sudden, Allison grabbed Mel's arm. She pointed at Diana's leg.

Mel's eyes opened wide. "Um, Diana," she said. "Don't panic when I say this, but don't move. And don't look down, okay?"

Chapter 17

Diana froze. "What?" she said. "What is it?"

"It's just a…um…leech," Mel said.

A squeak escaped Diana's lips.

Mel eyed the shiny black leech. It was sticking to Diana's leg like a huge gooey blob. "It's okay," she said. "Allison will just run up to camp and get some salt."

"Or I could get some matches," Allison said. "Then we could burn it off."

Diana squeaked again.

Mel pushed Allison toward the path. "Go! Get salt *and* matches."

"Hurry!" said Diana.

Allison ran up the path and disappeared.

Mel noticed that Diana was holding her breath. "Breathe!" she said. "You're going to pass out!"

"If I breathe, I might scream," Diana said.

"That would be okay," Mel said. "Go for it."

"I don't want to look like a wimp," Diana told her.

"Oh," said Mel. "I wouldn't worry about it in this case. No one likes leeches. And I have to say, that's the biggest leech I've ever seen."

Diana let out another squeak.

Finally, they heard the sound of footsteps. Mel looked up and saw Jake running down the path. Allison was right behind him.

"Oh, great," said Diana. "Just what I need."

"Stay calm," said Mel in a low voice.

"Holy cow!" said Jake, staring at Diana's leg. "That's huge!"

Allison took the salt out of his hand. "Less talk, more action," she said. She moved over beside Diana. Then she shook salt on the leech.

"Are you okay?" Jake asked Diana.

"Oh, I'm fine!" Diana's voice was a little higher than usual. "I've seen bigger leeches. This is nothing. Remember the one we saw on our last canoe trip?" She shot Mel a look.

"Er, yeah," said Mel. "That leech was bigger." She poked Allison in the ribs.

"What?" said Allison. "Oh, right. *That* leech. Yeah, it was bigger. Much bigger."

The leech suddenly curled up and fell off. It plopped onto the rock at Diana's feet. A spot of blood appeared on her leg. Allison put a bandage over the spot.

Mel bent down and flicked the leech into the lake. "It's gone," she said.

"Great," said Jake. "Good job. Now, you guys had better run up and get some breakfast. We have to get going soon. Mrs. Hill wants to leave early." He jogged back toward camp.

Mel and Allison started walking, too. Then Mel realized that Diana wasn't with them. She looked back. Diana was still standing in the same spot, frozen.

"Diana, you can move now," Allison called. "The big, scary leech is gone."

Mel and Allison ran back to Diana. Diana started to flap her hands and stomp her feet. Her mouth opened and closed, but no noise came out.

Mel and Allison looked at each other. "Should we slap her?" Allison asked.

"No!" Mel said quickly.

Allison put up her hands. "I was kidding."

By then, Diana had calmed down. "I'm okay. I'm okay. I'm okay," she kept saying.

They walked back toward camp.

"Was it really that big?" Diana asked.

"Didn't you look?" Mel said.

"You told me not to!" Diana said. "Besides, I didn't want to panic in front of Jake."

Allison laughed. "Come on, let's go eat."

"I don't have time for breakfast!" Diana said. "I have to get to the tent and do my hair."

"You have to eat!" Mel told her.

"Come on," Allison added. "You can do your hair after. Or you can just wear a hat!" She dragged Diana over to the eating area.

Mel went to their tent. She started to pack her bag. Jake came by to get their sleeping bags and sleeping pads. He took them down to the canoes. After a while, Allison came and got her backpack. "I'll meet you guys down at the lake," she told Mel.

"Let's go!" Mrs. Hill shouted across the campsite. "Meet at the canoes in five minutes!"

Mel put on a baseball cap. *Diana won't have time to do her hair,* she thought.

At that moment, Diana burst into the tent. She was out of breath. "Quick!" she whispered. She yanked a brush out of her backpack. She started brushing her hair with fast strokes.

"Come on, get packed. We have to go," Mel told her.

"No! I'm not ready!" Diana looked around wildly. "Pass me my little makeup bag!"

"I don't think you have time," Mel said.

"Yes, I do," Diana said, holding out her hand. She snapped her fingers. "Just pass me the bag."

Mel looked inside Diana's backpack. She pulled out a small bag. "Is this it?"

"No!" said Diana. "The green one."

Mel found the bag and tossed it to Diana. "Maybe you can get in Jake's canoe today."

Diana dropped the bag. All her makeup fell out. "Ahhh! Not looking like this, I can't. I look awful." She rushed to pick up her makeup.

"Let's go, girls!" Mrs. Hill poked her head into the tent. "Out! I need to pack up the tent. Everyone is waiting for you."

"Oh noooo!" Diana cried. Mel helped her stuff everything in her pack. Then the two girls took their bags and ran down to the lake.

Chapter 18

The group gathered by the canoes. Diana had pulled on a baseball hat. Mrs. Hill came down carrying the last of the gear. "Okay, listen up!" she said. "We are starting out early today. It's going to be a hot one. I don't want anyone passing out from heat stroke. Today we're going to paddle down Loon River. Then we'll portage over to Windy Lake. We'll cross the lake and camp there for the night."

"Life jackets!" Jake called. The boys ran to the canoes. Diana asked if she could go in Mrs. Hill's canoe.

Mel pulled Diana aside. "Why did you do that?" she asked. "You should have gone with Jake. That's why you came on this trip, right? Remember?"

Diana shook her head. "I couldn't do it. My hair is a mess. My hands have all these blisters. I look awful with no makeup on. I can't let Jake see me like this!"

Mel sighed. *Makeup is fine,* she thought. *But hello! Not when you're camping!* To Diana, she said, "You look really good, you know. Even with no makeup on. But whatever. Let's go."

Soon, the group was ready. Mel was sharing a canoe with Tetsuo and Patrick. They set off down the river behind Allison's canoe.

It was another sunny day. *Mrs. Hill was right,* Mel thought. *It's a hot one.* She took off her baseball hat and dunked it in the lake. Then she twisted it to get the water out. When she put the hat back on, her head felt much cooler. "Ahhhh," she said.

Patrick looked back and saw what Mel had done. He took off his own hat and dunked it in the lake. He didn't twist out the water. When he put the hat back on, water streamed down his neck. His T-shirt got wet, too. "Ahhh!" he said.

Tetsuo copied Patrick. "Eeeek!" he cried when the water ran down his back.

Mel smiled to herself. She paddled with steady strokes. The canoe slid through the water. Once in a while, she snacked on a bag of trail mix. *This is the life*, she thought. *There is only one thing that would make this trip better. Will. I wish he had come with us. And I wish we hadn't argued.*

Mel wondered what was going to happen when she got home. *I guess I'll just have to wait and find out. I'll be home tomorrow. At least if we break up, I'll have Diana to hang out with. Allison and Kyle can do stuff without me and Will.*

She looked back at her friend. Diana was paddling at the front of Mrs. Hill's canoe. *She looks like she's having an okay time*, Mel thought. *I think this trip was a good idea. Even if she doesn't get a date with Jake. Her parents told her she couldn't do it. Now she's proving them wrong.*

The morning went by quickly. They stopped for lunch and then rested while the sun was at its hottest. Diana shared some of her secret stash of snacks with Mel and Allison. "I'm saving two chocolate bars," she told them. "That and the cheese popcorn will get me through tomorrow."

"You're doing great," Allison told her.

Later in the day, they did the second part of the route. They set up camp on the far side of Windy Lake.

Jake cooked a pot of stew for dinner. Diana wrinkled her nose, but she ate two bowls of stew. "One more day and we can go home," she sighed. They roasted marshmallows for dessert. "These will give me zits," Diana said. But she ate them anyway.

Mel caught Diana stealing looks at Jake. The light from the fire danced across his face. Then he laughed at something Patrick said. Mel had to agree that he was pretty cute. He had a great smile. *He and Diana would look good together*, she thought to herself.

Once in a while, Mel caught Jake looking at Diana, too.

After dinner, all the campers helped clean up. Jake and Allison took the food bags away from the campsite. They hung them in the trees. Diana ran over and they hung up her pack, as well.

They didn't sing after dinner. Instead, Mrs. Hill told ghost stories. She was pretty good at it. Even Mel felt a bit nervous going back to her tent in the dark.

Chapter 19

Mel was so tired that she fell asleep right away. She dreamed that Will was standing on the shore of the lake. She paddled and paddled, but she couldn't get to him.

When she woke up the next morning, the tent was empty. *I must have slept in,* she thought. She peeked out of the tent. The food bags were still hanging up, so it wasn't time for breakfast. Mrs. Hill was leading some of the boys down to the lake.

Then Mel saw Allison running over to the tent. Diana was right behind her. She was carrying her backpack. *She must have taken it down from the trees,* Mel thought.

"Quick!" Allison called. "Get your bathing suit on!" She rushed into the tent and started changing. "Gordie saw a moose on the other side of the lake. We're all going down to look, and then we're going for a swim."

Diana dropped her backpack. She rolled her eyes and said, "Woohoo. A moose." But she pulled out her bathing suit anyway.

Mel quickly changed her clothes. The girls ran down to the lake. The rest of the group was standing near the canoes. The boys were talking and pointing across the lake. "There it is!" one of them said.

The moose was standing on the far side of the lake. Even from far away, it looked big. Mrs. Hill passed around her binoculars.

Then it was time to go swimming. Omar pointed to a small island. "Can we swim there and back?" he asked.

"No," said Jake. "That island is farther away than it looks." He pointed to a closer spot. "Let's swim to that little rock and back."

"Okay," said Omar. "I'll race you!" he shouted to the other boys. Then he splashed into the water. Jake and the other boys were right behind him.

Mel went for a swim. Then she offered to go with Mrs. Hill. It was time to get the food ready for breakfast. The two of them started walking back to camp. It was a short path through the trees. The camp soon came into sight.

All of a sudden, Mrs. Hill stopped walking. She put out her arm to stop Mel. "Did you hear that?" she whispered.

"What?" said Mel.

"Shhh," said Mrs. Hill. She moved behind a tree and pulled Mel with her. They were at the edge of the campsite.

Mel looked around. Nothing was moving. It was completely quiet. *Too quiet*, Mel thought.

Then she heard a loud noise. It sounded like a grunt. Her eyes opened wide. She looked at Mrs. Hill. Mrs. Hill frowned.

They couldn't see anything. The noise came again. *That was clearly a grunt*, thought Mel.

The noise was coming from the yellow tent. All of a sudden, the sides of the tent started moving. It looked like something large was inside. Something very large. Then Mel heard a ripping noise and a growl.

"Is that what I think it is?" Mel whispered.

"Let's not wait to find out," said Mrs. Hill.

Chapter 20

"Let's get back down to the lake," said Mrs. Hill. "If it's a bear, we don't want it to see us."

They started walking back down the path. Then they started to run. It didn't take long to reach the shore. Diana and Allison were sitting on the rocks, chatting.

"I don't want to cause a panic," Mrs. Hill told the girls. She spoke in a low voice. "We need to hurry. Diana, Mel, untie the canoes. Get them in the water. Allison, you get the paddles. I'll get the boys' attention. I want everyone in the boats right away. We will paddle over to that island."

"What's going on?" Allison asked.

"Bear!" Mel whispered. Diana and Allison stared at her in shock. "Maybe!" Mel added.

"Move it, girls!" Mrs. Hill hissed.

They worked as fast as they could. Mrs. Hill gave a loud whistle. She waved Jake back to shore. Then she told him what was going on. The girls got the boats ready. Diana handed out life jackets. Jake got the boys into the canoes. Mrs. Hill told them it was a game. They were going to paddle over to the rocky island. But they had to be as quiet as possible.

The group made it to the small island in record time. They pulled the canoes up onto the rocks. "Keep your life jackets on!" Mrs. Hill told them. Then she climbed up a small hill. She had her binoculars around her neck.

All the campers followed her. They went up to the highest point on the island. Mrs. Hill raised the binoculars to her eyes.

"Can you see the camp?" Jake asked.

"Yes," she replied.

"Can you see if it's a bear?" Mel asked.

All the boys started talking at once.

"A bear!"

"What?"

"Can I see?"

"Where?"

"Let me look!"

"Quiet!" shouted Mel. She looked at Mrs. Hill and waited.

"It *is* a bear," Mrs. Hill reported. "He's ripped a big hole in the yellow tent."

Allison, Mel, and Diana looked at one another. "That's our tent!" Allison whispered.

"The bear is holding a backpack," Mrs. Hill said.

Mel realized she was holding her breath.

Diana slapped her hand over her mouth. "Uh oh," she whispered.

"He's ripping that, too," Mrs. Hill said. "Now he's eating something…I can't quite see what…"

Diana let out a tiny cry.

"I can see it now," said Mrs. Hill. "It looks like a bag of…popcorn. He's eating it, even the bag. And something else that I can't see."

"Chocolate bars." Diana's voice was a choked whisper. "Chocolate bars." She closed her eyes.

Allison put her arm around Diana.

Diana's eyes filled with tears. "This is my fault," she said.

"It's okay. We're safe," Mel said. "No one got hurt."

Diana wrapped her arms around her knees. She didn't say a word.

Mrs. Hill passed the binoculars around to the boys. They all wanted to see the bear. Mel and Allison sat with Diana. Jake stood nearby.

Mrs. Hill stood up and looked at the group. She put her hands on her hips. "Okay, folks, we are all safe. That's good." Her voice became stern. "But listen up. This is why we don't keep food in our tents. We asked you not to bring food with you. It is a danger. Someone could have been hurt. I hope you've all learned an important lesson from this."

"It's my fault," Diana said quietly. She let out a small sob. "I'm not a camper! I can't do anything right. I hate being dirty." She stood up. "And I almost got us all killed!" She started to run across the rocks. She was headed for the other side of the island.

Mel and Allison started to run after her.

"Wait!" said Jake. "Let me talk to Diana."

Chapter 21

Allison looked at Mel. Mel shrugged. They both stood and watched Jake run after Diana.

Mrs. Hill called them over. "The bear is gone," she said. "It finished its snack and took off into the trees. Now, I'm going over to pack up the gear. Alone. I'm sure it's safe now, but I don't want to take any chances. I'll bring everything down to the shore. Then you can send Jake over to pick it up. I want you to stay here with the boys."

"I can help pick up the stuff," Allison said.

"Thank you, Allison," Mrs. Hill said. "But no. Jake and I are in charge of this trip. I want to make sure everyone stays safe. So we will take care of the gear. You have been a big help already."

The girls watched Mrs. Hill climb down the rocks. Soon she was paddling across the lake.

Allison took the boys down to the water to skip rocks. Mel stayed and watched Mrs. Hill to make sure nothing went wrong. After a while, Jake and Diana came back. Diana's face was wet with tears, but she was smiling. Jake had his arm around her shoulder.

"Hi, guys," Mel said. She explained Mrs. Hill's plan. Then she took another look with the binoculars. "There's a bunch of gear ready to be picked up," she told Jake.

He nodded. "I'm on my way." He put his hand on Diana's shoulder. "Will you be okay?"

Diana nodded. Jake started climbing down the rocks. "Be careful," Diana called to him.

Mel waited until Jake was gone. Then she turned to look at Diana. Her friend had a big smile on her face. "Okay, spill it," said Mel.

"I told him the truth," Diana said.

"The *whole* truth?" Mel asked.

"Yeah. I told him that I'm a big fake. And that I only came on this trip because I thought he was cute."

Mel raised her eyebrows. "Really?"

Diana nodded. "Yes. And guess what!"

"What?"

"Jake doesn't really like camping, either," Diana said.

"What!" Mel said. "Get out of here."

"Yeah," said Diana. "He's done it before, of course. But he only knows the basics. And get this! Jake was nervous around *me!* He thought I knew so much about camping." She laughed. "He even read up about it before we came. He didn't want me to think he wasn't a good camper."

Mel laughed, too. She remembered the day she had signed up for the trip. Jake had been reading a book when she came in. He had stuffed it in a drawer. It must have been a book about camping. "What is Jake doing leading a camping trip, then?" Mel asked.

"Well, Mrs. Hill is the real leader of the trip. Jake is just doing this job because he works at the hotel. Mr. Magee wants him to start from the ground up. He wants Jake to learn all the parts of the business. Even the summer program. Jake wants to go to business school. He wants to help run the hotel someday."

"Who knew?" said Mel. Then she thought of something else. "Hey, that means Jake liked you all along!"

Diana grinned. "Yeah. He thought I liked someone else, thanks to Allison. But he knows the truth now. He asked me to go out for dinner after we get back."

"No way!" said Mel.

"And he told me that they're building a pool at the hotel."

Mel laughed. "So you'll never have to swim in the lake again."

"Never," said Diana. "I won't have to go camping again, either."

"Come on," said Mel. "Are you telling me you didn't have fun? Look how much you learned! And you've proved to your parents that you can do it."

"I know," said Diana. "It was a dumb idea in the first place. But I'm glad I came. I did learn stuff, thanks to you. And now I know I can do it. But I also know that it's not really my thing."

"You might be right about that," Mel said.

They looked at each other and laughed.

Chapter 22

Jake and Mrs. Hill got all the gear. They brought it back to the small island. The yellow tent was destroyed. So was Diana's backpack. Diana felt awful about it. She told Mel she would buy her a new backpack. She promised to buy a new tent, too. She told the group she was sorry a million times. Finally, Allison offered to toss her in the lake.

They ate a quick breakfast on the island. Mrs. Hill repacked the gear. Jake loaded and tied it into the canoes. Then Mrs. Hill spoke to the group. "I think we've had enough adventure for one trip. It's a good thing we're on our way home today. Let's go!"

The boys cheered. Then they piled into the canoes. The group set off across Windy Lake. The boys in Mel's canoe couldn't stop talking about the bear. Diana and Jake shared one of the canoes.

Diana looks happy, Mel thought. *For once, she doesn't seem to care that her hair is messy. She doesn't have makeup on, either.*

It took five hours to reach the end of their route. They landed on the far side of Lake Sumac. Mel's arms were tired as she pulled her canoe up onto the sandy beach.

Mr. Hill was waiting for them in a big van. He had a trailer ready for the canoes.

"Okay, folks!" Mrs. Hill said. "My husband will drive us back to Deer Lake in the van. Your parents will pick you up at the public dock."

Mr. and Mrs. Hill put the canoes on the trailer. Jake loaded camping gear into the van.

At last they were ready to go. The van was stuffed full. The boys told Mr. Hill all about their trip as he drove to Deer Lake.

It was a short trip. Some parents were waiting at the dock when the van pulled up. The boys jumped out in a rush. Jake and the Hills greeted the boys' parents.

Allison's brother, Ian, drove up in a blue pickup truck. He waved to the girls. Allison gave Mel a hug good-bye. Then she hugged Diana. "You did all right, you know," she said.

Diana rolled her eyes. "Yeah, whatever!" she said. They all laughed.

Allison picked up her bag and got in the truck. She leaned out the window as they drove away. "See you guys tomorrow!"

Yes! thought Mel. *I think my friendship plan worked! Who knew?*

Diana looked at Mel. "Can I get a ride home with you?" she asked.

"Sure," said Mel. "I think I see my dad's minivan coming."

The Hills came over to say good-bye. "I'll pay for the tent," Diana promised again. Mrs. Hill gave her a hug.

Diana turned to Mel. "Please tell your dad I'll buy a new backpack," she said. Then Diana ran over to say good-bye to Jake. The two of them stood talking and holding hands.

Mr. Randall drove up. Mel picked up her backpack and started walking. Then she stopped. Someone was getting out of the minivan. It wasn't her dad.

It was Will.

He walked down the dock to meet her. His hands were in his pockets. "Hey," he said.

"Hey," said Mel.

They were both quiet for a second. Then they both spoke at once.

"Sorry! I—"

"I was worried—"

Will smiled, and then he looked at the ground. "I'm sorry I got mad at you before," he said. "I wanted to go on the canoe trip, but I couldn't. I didn't want to ask my mom for the money. I was too ashamed to tell you."

Mel's mouth dropped open. *Oh no!* she thought. *I should have thought of that. I know his mom doesn't have a lot of money. Here I was thinking he didn't want to hang out with me.*

"I'm sorry, too," she told Will. "I should have known. I should have asked. I hated thinking you were mad at me."

Will pulled one hand out of his pocket. He handed Mel a hemp bracelet. "I made this for you," he said shyly.

Mel took the bracelet. It was a bit uneven and a bit too big. But she loved it. She held out her arm. "Can you put it on me?" she asked.

Will grinned. He tied the bracelet for Mel. "It's not as good as the ones you make."

"It's perfect," Mel said.

Will picked up her backpack. "Let's go."

"Wait! We have to get Diana," Mel said.

"No, we don't," said Will. He pointed. A fancy black car had pulled up to the dock. Diana stood beside it, talking to her parents. Jake was shaking her dad's hand.

Mel waved good-bye to them. Will climbed into the back seat of the minivan. Then Mel got in the front seat. "Hi, Dad," she said.

"Hi, kiddo," he said. "Ready to go home?"

"Oh yeah," said Mel.

"So how was the trip?" asked Mr. Randall.

"It's a long story," said Mel. "A *verrrrry* long story."

"I was going to ask you to go canoeing later," said Will. "Does that mean you won't want to go?"

Mel groaned. "I need a day off. Let's just hang out and play cards or something."

Will grinned. "Okay. We have the rest of the summer to go canoeing."

Mel grinned back. "Yeah, we do, don't we?"

Glossary

biodegradable
Describing something that will break down
safely and will not harm the environment

canoe
A light, narrow boat that is paddled

conservation area
A natural area, such as a forest, in which people
are not allowed to build houses or roads

cottage
A small house that is used for vacation

first aid
Care given to a person who is ill or hurt

hemp
A type of plant that is used to make rope
or cloth

heron
A large, long-necked bird

leech
A kind of bloodsucking worm found in fresh water

loon
A type of water bird

portage
To carry a boat over land

sleeping pad
A soft pad that is placed under a sleeping bag

speedboat
A motorboat that can travel very quickly

sunblock
A lotion or cream used to block harmful rays from the sun and prevent sunburn

Thailand
A country located in Asia

trail mix
A snack mix of nuts, seeds, and dried fruit

waterskiing
A water sport in which a person is pulled behind a boat while on skis

Special Thanks

...to Haley MacRae, Sam Turton, Janet Lewis, and Paul Lewis, for taking the time to read this manuscript and give me feedback.

...to Kornel Strzalkowski (and helpers Kate and Patrick) for reading the manuscript and sharing your knowledge of camping and canoe trips.

...to Bob Holmes and Harriet Geller for their input on the title.

...to Kerri Wall for her vocabulary help.

...and to Ben Kooter and the Tea Leaves!